The
Creative
Tao

PAMELA K. METZ

The Creative Tao

Pamela K. Metz

Humanics Trade
PO Box 7400
Atlanta, GA 30357

The Creative Tao
A Humanics Publication

Copyright ©1997 by Humanics Limited

No part of this book may be reproduced or transmitted in any form or by any means, electronic or mechanical, including photocopying, recording, or by any information storage and retrieval system, without permission in writing from the publisher. For information address: Humanics Limited.

Library of Congress Cataloging-in-Publication Data
Metz, Pamela. 1940-
    The Creative Tao: an art of living/ Pamela K. Metz.— 1st ed.
    p. cm.
    ISBN 0-89334-255-6
    1. Tao. 2. Philosophy, Taoist. 3. Lao Tzu. Tao te ching.
    I. Lao Tzu. Tao te ching. 1996. II. Title.
B127.T3M45 1997
181'. 114—DC21   96-48365
                                                                                    CIP

Published simultaneously in the United States and Canada

Humanics Trade Publications are an imprint of and published by Humanics Limited, a division of Humanics Publishing Group, Inc. Its trademark, consisting of the words "Humanics Trade" and the portrayal of a Pegasus, is Registered in U.S. Patent and Trademark Office and in other countries. Humanics Limited, P.O. Box 7400, Atlanta, GA 30309.

Printed in the United States of America

It is not a question of an artist being a special kind of person,

but of every person being a special kind of artist.

COOMARASWAMY

The most visible creators I know of are

those artists whose medium is life itself.

The ones who express the inexpressible -

without brush, hammer, clay or guitar.

They neither paint nor sculpt -

their medium is being. Whatever their presence

touches has increased life. They see and

don't have to draw. They are the artists

of being alive.

STONE

Table of Contents

Acknowledgments

I thank my family, friends, colleagues, and students for their steadfast support through my own unfolding discoveries of creative ways. I am pleased to work with Gary Wilson of Humanics Publishing who continues to bring Tao books to readers.

Introduction

Lao Tzu, according to tradition, was born in China in 570 B.C.E. When or where he died, and even if he ever lived at all, remains unknown. The name *Lao* translates to ancient or venerable, and *Tzu* represents a respectful term similar to Sir or Master. The Tao Te Ching attributed to him probably represents a compilation of important philosophical ideals, acquired over time, from various great minds.

The legends surrounding his life and works trace back to a historical event; the Chou Dynasty, which lasted from c. 1100- 200 B.C.E., was plagued with inner turmoil. The resulting factions and civil wars are reflected in the dozens of philosophies also competing during this time. Taoism, judging by its lasting effects, was the most victorious.

The word *Tao* can be explained simply as 'the way', but there is such a deeper meaning embodied within the *Tao* that there is no simple translation. *Te* means the appropriate use of human life by humans, and *Ching* translates to book, or collection. The vast array of Taoist works continues to be expanded, with modern interpretations transforming the ancient Tao into a timeless entity.

道可道非常道名可名非常名無名天地之始

有名萬物之母故常無欲以觀其妙

常有欲以觀其徼此兩者同出而異名

同謂之元元之又元眾妙之門

Before the Beginning:
Getting Started

To create is to struggle with the empty spaces
of the canvas,
the blank page,
or the void of the empty stage.

To live is to do the same.

Before the shapes take form, there is the nothingness.
There must be nothingness before the beginning.

Before the beginning is prologue:
all that has come before.

天下皆知美之為美斯惡已皆知善之為善斯不善已
故有無相生難易相成長短相較高下相傾音聲相和
前後相隨是以聖人處無為之事行不言之教
萬物作焉而不辭生而不有為而不恃功成而弗居
夫唯弗居是以不去

2

Conundrums

What perspective to take? Some people see things this way
and others that way.

Creating and living are not separate.
Creating comes in everyday living.

The creative person waits and writes.

Without the words, images, music, and forms, nothing lasts.
With the words, images, music, and forms, what is forgotten?

It is important to keep a record of your people.
It is important to remember, even if the record is incomplete.

不尚賢使民不爭不貴難得之貨
使民不為盜不見可欲使民心不亂
是以聖人之治虛其心實其腹弱其志
強其骨常使民無知無欲
使夫智者不敢為也 為無為則無不治

Mentors

When you think too much of great artists,
you may lose some self-regard.
If you only collect others' ideas, you may lose your own.

A good mentor guides by trusting and by motivating others.
A mentor makes a place for growth to happen.

Not creating creates the places for creativity to appear.

道冲而用之或不盈淵兮
似萬物之宗挫其銳解其紛
和其光同其塵湛兮似或存
吾不知誰之子象帝之先

Creativity

Creativity is a gift to every human being.

It is never used up and is always available.

No one knows where it is, or where it goes.

One only needs to trust, and there it is!

天地不仁以萬物為芻狗聖人不仁
以百姓為芻狗天地之間其猶橐籥乎
虛而不屈動而愈出多言數窮不如守中

5

From the Heart

The Tao holds all things, both beneficial and dangerous.
The artist, too, has tools to create both goodness and badness.

The heart of the matter determines how the creating evolves.

The more you create, the more creativity is available.
The more honest the feelings, the truer the forms.

Create from the heart.

谷神不死 是謂元牝 元牝之門
是謂天地根 緜緜若存 用之不勤

源 The Right Ways

The Right Ways

The Tao is the mother of all things:
it gives life away, yet it remains full of life.

Creativity, like the Tao, is always available.

You can find the right ways whenever you want.

Your own way is the right way to creative living.

Creativity 因

天長地久天地所以能長且久者以其不自生

故能長生是以聖人後其身而身先

外其身而身存非以其無私耶故能成其私

連

Taking Your Time

14

7

Taking Your Time

Creating takes time. Why is this?

The words cannot form themselves on the page.
The words and shapes and forms have no meaning without
the direction of the creator.

A writer seems slow, and yet the story is written.

She does not claim fame, yet the words are known to be hers.

When she takes her time, she lets go and the stories unfold.

Creativity 因

上善若水水善利萬物而不爭

處眾人之所惡故幾於道居善地心善淵

與善仁言善信政善治事善能

動善時夫唯不爭故無尤

流 Courage

8

Courage

To live a creative life, be like water;
nourish your ideas in their infancy.

When you create,
Stay close to your sources.
Keep your ideas true to their meanings.
Maintain the truth as you know it.
Trust those who follow to find their way.
Enjoy your process.
Have courage to be present to the creating.

When you have the courage to create your own life,
it will no longer matter who judges your way of living.

持而盈之不如其已揣而梲之不可長保

金玉滿堂莫之能守富貴而驕

自遺其咎功遂身退天下之道

滿 Rewards

9

Rewards

Creating is its own reward.

Only you can make your world be known.
If you care only for money and fame,
you will never be content.
If you rely only on others' praise,
you will not recognize yourself.

Create what you must, then stop.

This is the only way to contentment.

載營魄抱一能無離乎專氣致柔能嬰兒乎

滌除元覽能無疵乎愛民治國能無知乎

天門開闔能無雌乎明白四達能無為乎

生之畜之生而不有為而不恃

長而不宰是謂元德

Re-Visioning

Can you allow your vision to revise itself?
Can you let go of this color and then choose that one?
Can you delete words without adding more
until the way is found?
Can you let the story write itself?
Can you separate yourself from the creating in order to
experience it as new?

Creating without owning,
revising without sorrow,
this process leads to new possibilities.

三十輻共一轂當其無有車之用

埏埴以為器當其無有器之用

鑿戶牖以為室當其無有室之用

故有之以為利無之以為用

11

Mistakes

We draw lines on the paper,
but the empty spaces make the images emerge.

We put covers on a book,
but the beginnings and endings come from the source.

We work with materials, space and sound,
but the creative person
creates from the spirit and meaning of them all.

Mistakes teach us to begin again, learning to keep trying.

五色令人目盲五音令人耳聾

五味令人口爽馳騁畋獵令人心發狂

難得之貨令人行妨是以聖人為腹不為目

故去彼取此

12

Timing

Creating comes in its own time.

A story of age cannot be written in youth.
An ending may come before a beginning.

The creative person lives in the world
but listens to his inner speech.

He allows the world to unfold
while opening to the feelings of his own heart.

寵辱若驚貴大患若身何謂寵辱若驚

寵為下得之若驚失之若驚是謂寵辱若驚

何謂貴大患若身吾所以有大患者為吾有身

及吾無身吾有何患故貴以身為天下

若可寄天下愛以身為天下若可託天下

13

In the Nature of Things

It is in the nature of things to fail and to succeed.
Is one of these better than another?

Whether you are creating or not creating,
the outcome is uncertain.
When you remember *why* you create,
you will be in harmony with the way things are.

What does it mean to fail or to succeed?
Who decides these things?

If we do not focus on the self, then we are free to discover.
The nature of things is how we are.

When we create, there is no success or failure.
There is just creation. There is just the Tao.

視之不見名曰夷聽之不聞名曰希搏之不得名曰微

此三者不可致詰故混而為一其上不皦其下不昧

繩繩不可名復歸於無物是謂無狀之狀無物之象

是謂惚恍迎之不見其首隨之不見其後

執古之道以御今之有能知古始是謂道紀

14

Beyond the Forms

Words cannot capture all there is.
Colors are also limited.
Much that matters in life cannot be grasped.

When creating, reach beyond the forms to the meanings
behind them. Remember that others know this as well.

When we understand that creativity is like a cloud,
(you can see it, but cannot touch it),
then we can be at peace with the limits of our work.

古之善為士者微妙元通深不可識夫唯不可識

故強為之容豫焉若冬涉川猶兮若畏四鄰

儼兮其若容渙兮若冰之將釋敦兮其若樸曠兮

其若谷混兮其若濁孰能濁以靜之徐清

孰能安以久動之徐生保此道者不欲盈夫唯不盈

故能蔽不新成

慧 Other Artists

30

15

Other Artists

Many artists have made their marks. The creations they have
left us are profound,
> and funny,
> and sad,
> and beautiful,
> and ugly,
> and true,
> and untrue.

They gave us what they could.
They left us what was available.

Can you be patient with your own process?
Can you be receptive until your work demands to take form?

The creative person does not expect to be like others.
When she trusts her process,
she can create in her own true way.

She creates in the spirit of the Tao.

致虛極守靜篤萬物並作吾以觀復夫物芸芸

各復歸其根歸根曰靜是謂復命復命曰常知常曰明

不知常妄作凶知常容容乃公公乃王

王乃天天乃道道乃久沒身不殆

环 From the Depths

16

From the Depths

Make yourself empty and full of peace.
Be mindful of others and keep a place for them in your life.

Each person has access to his own authentic being.

Each person is creative in his own unique way.

When people forget that they are creative,
they lose sight of their possibilities.

When you remember the creative Tao,
you make a life that is ready when death approaches.

太上下知有之其次親而譽之

其次畏之其次侮之

信不足焉有不信焉

悠兮其貴言功成事遂百姓皆謂我自然

産

The Creative Leader

The Creative Leader

When a leader is creative, others are unaware of him.
There are also leaders who are loved.
Some leaders are feared and a few are hated.
When people are not trusted by their leaders,
they become untrustworthy.

The creative leader doesn't talk about his creativity; he lives it.
When his work becomes visible,
others take it for granted and say
that it was there all of the time!

Creativity 因

大道廢有仁義慧智出有大偽

六親不和有孝慈國家皆乱有忠臣

 Despair

18

Despair

When the creative Tao is lost,
sameness and mass production appear.

When inner wisdom is forgotten,
outer conformity and stereotypes become evident.

When a family loses its creativity,
the members worry about its health.
When our country is confused,
substitutions for originality suffice.

絕聖棄智民利百倍絕仁棄義民復孝慈

絕巧棄利盜賊無有此三者以為文不足

故令有所屬見素抱樸少私寡欲

涌 Deliverance

19

Deliverance

When people let go of goals and expectations,
they will find the source of their own creativity.
If not directed by others, they will find the best thing to do.

When profit and machinery are less important,
people become more creative.

If deliverance from these is not possible,
stay centered in your own resourcefulness and follow
the creative Tao.

絕學無憂唯之與阿相去幾何善之與惡相去若何

人之所畏不可不畏荒兮其未央哉

眾人熙熙如享太牢如春登臺我獨泊兮其未兆

如嬰兒之未孩儽儽兮若無所歸眾人皆餘而我獨若遺

我愚人之心也哉沌沌兮俗人昭昭我獨昏昏

俗人察察我獨悶悶澹兮其若海飂兮若無止

眾人皆有以而我獨頑似鄙我獨異於人而貴食母

独 Loneliness

20

Loneliness

Creating your own life sometimes means feeling lonely.
Why is this so?

When others watch sporting events or are constantly busy,
the creative person may not join in.

There are periods of time where no creative way appears.
These lonely times provide the emptiness into which
the creative juices flow.
These are the times to remember the Tao.

Fill your empty spaces with the creative Tao.

孔德之容惟道是從道之為物惟恍惟惚

惚兮恍兮其中有象恍兮惚兮其中有物

窈兮冥兮其中有精其精甚真其中有信

自古及今其名不去以閱眾甫

吾何以知眾甫之狀哉以此

思 Development

21

Development

When living, keep the creative Tao in mind.
This will give you hope.

Even though the Tao cannot be held,
it helps in the creative process.

Out of the mystery, a creative way becomes clearer.

How do we know this?
Look inside and find your own creative way.

曲則全枉則直窪則盈敝則新少則得多則惑

是以聖人抱一為天式不自見故明不自是故彰不自伐故有功

不自矜故長夫唯不爭故天下莫能與之爭

古之所謂曲則全者豈虛言哉誠全而歸之

22

Purpose

To find your creative ways, let go of seeking them.

If your purpose in life is to be like others,
you will not find the way that is yours alone.

Let go of the "expected" way and
find the unfolding purpose in your life.
Give up following others' ways and open to your own.

It is only by being true to your path
that you create your own way.
The creative Tao then becomes your own true self.

希言自然故飄風不終朝驟雨不終日孰為此者天地

天地尚不能久而況於人乎

故從事於道者同於道德者同於德失者同於失

同於道者道亦樂得之同於德者德亦樂得之

同於失者失亦樂得之信不足焉有不信焉

23

Persistence

Do not give up too soon.
Do it your way and then step back.

Stay with your ideas until they take form.
If you embrace the creative Tao,
you become one with your ideas.
You can express them as they take you on your journey.

Become receptive to the creative Tao and trust your responses.
Your life becomes what it must,
and the pieces fall into their natural places.

企者不立跨者不行自見者不明

自是者不彰自伐者無功

自矜者不長其在道也曰

餘食贅行物或惡之故有道者不處

已 Just Do It!

24

Just Do It!

If you paint with colors but cannot enjoy it;

If you write the words, and they are not the truth;

If you dance, and your muscles won't follow;

If you sing, and the lyrics stick to your tongue;

If you cannot find your creative forms;

Let go of this and wait for that.

When you are in harmony with the creative Tao,
just do it, and then let go.

有物混成先天地生

寂兮寥兮獨立不改周行而不殆可以為天下母

吾不知其名字之曰道強為之名曰大

大曰逝逝曰遠遠曰反故道大天大地大王亦大

域中有四大而王居其一焉人法地地法天天法道道法自然

Incubation

Before ideas take shape, there is a period of incubation.
There must be time for rest, for growth, for dreaming.

This incubation is necessary in nature and in creativity.

After the beginning of the idea and before the idea takes form,
the creative Tao moves through the necessary stages
and evolves into itself.

重為輕根靜為躁君

是以聖人終日行不離輜重雖有榮觀燕處超然

奈何萬乘之主而以身輕天下輕則失本躁則失君

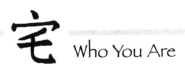

宅 Who You Are

26

Who You Are

Emptiness gives birth to substance.
Uncertainty comes before form.

Like the turtle,
the creative person is at home wherever she is.
She knows that creating is an extension of herself.
She is not flattered by others' opinions
but continues her work as she must.

If you rush, trying to please others with your creative energies,
you forget your roots.
If you cannot follow your own creative way,
you lose sight of who you are.

Creativity 因

善行無轍迹善言無瑕讁善數不用籌策

善閉無關楗而不可開善結無繩約而不可解

是以聖人常善救人故無棄人常善救物故無棄物

是謂襲明故善人者不善人之師

不善人者善人之資不貴其師

不愛其資雖智大迷是謂要妙

行 What Is

54

27

What Is

An explorer works without a map,
and the journey is the destination.
A creative person trusts the unknown
and follows his intuitions.
The inventor forgets what has come before
and keeps an open mind.

Staying open to what is, is a secret for creative people.
They can experience whatever appears and waste nothing.
This is called embracing what is.

People who can use everything in life
help show others some possible ways.

If you do not understand this,
you cannot find your own way, even if you are very wise.

This is the secret of what is.

知其雄守其雌為天下谿為天下谿常德不離復歸於嬰兒

知其白守其黑為天下式為天下式常德不忒復歸於無極

知其榮守其辱為天下谷為天下谷常德乃足復歸於樸

樸散則為器聖人用之則為官長故大制不割

反 Balance

28

Balance

It is important to balance both male and female energies
in your daily living.
If you do this, you are with the creative Tao.

You should be aware of evil,
yet keep to the good and be a model for the world.
If you create a way of living that informs others,
you will be living the creative Tao.

Be aware of yourself, yet seek to know others,
accepting them as they are.
If you can do this,
you will find balance and be centered in the Tao.

A creative life is formed from nothingness,
like clouds in the sky.
The creative person knows the clouds and the sky
and appreciates them in their mystery.

Creativity 因

將欲取天下而為之吾見其不得已

天下神器不可為也為者敗之執者失之

故物或行或隨或歔或吹或強或羸或挫或隳

是以聖人去甚去奢去泰

 Seasons of the Circle

58

29

Seasons of the Circle

Do you want to change your life? How would you do this?
Your life was given to you. You did not choose it.
Keep it safe and nourish the gifts you were given.

There is a season for everything in life.

There is a time to move forward and a time to stay in place;
there is a time for leading and time to follow;
a time for activity and a time for resting;
a time to be secure and a time to take risks.

The creative person embraces things as they are
and lets them be themselves.
She watches as they follow their own cycles and transformations.
She lives through the seasons of her circle.

以道佐人主者不以兵強天下其事好還

師之所處荊棘生焉大軍之後必有凶年善有果而已不敢以取強

果而勿矜果而勿伐果而勿驕果而不得已果而勿強

物壯則老是謂不道不道早已

勇

When to Stop

30

When to Stop

When you follow the creative Tao,
you do not try to force ideas or impose them on others.

Wherever there is force, there is also resistance.

Even well-intentioned mandates can backfire on the creator.

The creative person creates and then stops.
She knows that the possibilities are infinite
and she does not try to control everything.
Trying to control is not being with the creative Tao.

When you have faith in yourself,
you don't need to influence others.
When you are happy with yourself,
you are not dependent on others' praise.
When you know when to stop, you are content in your life.

夫佳兵者不祥之器物或惡之故有道者不處

君子居則貴左用兵則貴右兵者不祥之器非君子之器

不得已而用之恬淡為上勝而不美而美之者是樂殺人

夫樂殺人者則不可以得志於天下矣吉事尚左凶了尚右

偏將軍居左將軍居右言以喪礼処之

殺人之眾以哀悲泣之戰勝以喪礼処之

静 Ideas

31

Ideas

Ideas are the seeds of creativity and should be cultivated.
When an idea appears, give it a home in which to develop.
Be gentle with it as it takes its uncertain form.

When creativity is valued, ideas will flourish.
When oppression is practiced, ideas remain a secret.

Living a creative life is available to everyone,
even while imprisoned.
Inner and outer creativity depend on the context.

Make a home for your ideas, wherever you are.

道常無名樸雖小天下莫能臣也侯王若能守之萬物將自賓

天地相合以降甘露民莫之令而自均

始制有名名亦既有夫亦將知止知止可以不殆

譬道之在天下猶川谷之於江海

32

Beyond Forms

The creative Tao is formless.
Though it is invisible, it contains infinite forms.

When women and men become aware of the Tao,
they promote harmony, and our world can become
a receptive place with peace and love at its center.

All forms are temporary.

A mountain is worn by the river;
the shoreline shrinks from the lapping of the sea.
Creations of music, dance, paintings and sculpture eventually
are forgotten, lost or destroyed.

Knowing that creating is beyond forms
frees you to make all forms.

Nothing lasts forever.
Everything returns to the Tao as trees surrender their leaves
to the earth at the end of autumn.

知人者智自知者明勝人者有力自勝者強

知足者富強行者有志不失其所者久死而不亡者壽

妳 Inspiration

33

Inspiration

Valuing others' creations may be inspiring.
Valuing your own work leads to wisdom.

Knowing others provides perspective.
Knowing yourself creates power.

When you know that enough is a feast,
you will always be satisfied.
When you maintain breath for your spirit
and embody life in all that you do,
your fears of death will diminish.

大道泛兮其可左右万物恃之而生而不辞功成不名有

衣养万物而不为主常无欲可名于小

万物归焉而不为主可名为大

以其终不自为大故能成其大

迷 Infinite Possibilities

34

Infinite Possibilities

The creative Tao is everywhere.
Everything comes from it,
yet the Tao does not create everything.

It is in every work, but it doesn't own the work.
It supports all creative efforts, but it doesn't hold on to them.

Since it is a part of creative living,
it doesn't draw attention to itself.
Because it holds infinite possibilities, it survives all forms.

It is not aware of itself; therefore,
it remains hidden in its humbleness.

Creativity 因

执大象天下往往而不害安平太乐与饵过客止

道之出口淡乎其无味视之不足见听之不足闻用之不足既

路 Travel(ing)

35

Travel (ing)

Someone who is one with the Tao can travel near and far.
She is aware of belonging to the universe, even when there is
pain and sorrow, because this is all part of the journey.

The warmth of the sun and the beauty of roses
may cause people to pause and take notice.
Words that describe creativity
may be lacking in vision and truth.

If you look for the Tao, you cannot see it.
If you listen for it, there is no sound.

If you use the Tao in creating,
there is always more than you need.

将欲歙之必固張之将欲弱之必固强之

将欲廢之必固興之将欲奪之必固與之

是謂微明柔弱勝剛強魚不可脫於淵

國之利器不可以示人

Mystery

Why is it that, in order to have something,
you must first give it up?
To get rid of something, you must first embrace it?
To create something, you must forget about creation?

This is the mystery of the creative Tao.

The gentle wins over the harsh,
and the reluctant surpasses the aggressive.
Let your creative process remain a mystery.
People can understand only the results.

道常無為而無不為侯王若能守之

萬物將自化化而欲作吾將鎮之以無名之樸

無名之樸夫亦將無欲不欲以靜天下將自正

Practice

The creative Tao does nothing,
yet all things are done through it.

If women and men would practice creative living,
then our world would be more natural.

People would find the artistry in their daily lives and be
surprised by their inventiveness.

When creativity is practiced,
there is contentment in the world.

上德不德是以有德下德不失德是以無德

上德無為而無以為下德為之而有以為

上仁為之而無以為上義為之而有以為上禮為之而莫之應

則攘臂而扔之故失道而後德失德而後仁失仁而後義失義而後禮

夫禮者忠信之薄而亂之首前識者道之華而愚之始是以大丈夫處其厚

不居其薄處其實不居其華故去彼取此

創 Creator/Creating

76

38

Creator/Creating

The creative person does not have to be an artist,
yet he provides art in living.

Some people contrive their lives and are often dissatisfied.

The creative person lets life flow but leaves nothing unfinished.

Some people are always busy and wish they had more time.

Out of chaos and uncertainty, the creative person
concerns himself with making a meaningful life.

He is the creator creating,
even when he does not know this is so.

昔之得一者天得一以清地得一以寧神得一以靈谷得一以盈萬物得一以生

侯王得一以為天下貞其致之天無以清將恐裂地無寧將恐發神無以靈

將恐歇谷無以盈將恐竭萬物無以生將恐滅侯王無以貴高將恐蹶

故貴以賤為本高以下為基是以侯王自謂孤寡不穀此非以賤為本耶

非乎故致數輿無輿不欲琭琭如玉珞珞如石

39

Repetition

When the creative Tao is honored,
life is good and there is harmony.

All creatures belong to the earth
and create the continuing story.
Happy with this balance,
there is endless repetition and renewal.

Interference with the way things are creates
disequilibrium, disharmony and disappointment.

When there is compassion for the parts because of their
importance to the whole,
the creative person can practice repetition.

With each repetition, there is change.
The artist becomes shaped by the Tao,
and her life is lived in a creative way.

反者道之動弱者道之用
天下萬物生於有有生於無

40

Silences

The creative Tao welcomes silence.
Listening is the way of the Tao.

Words come of silence.
Silence welcomes words.

上士聞道勤而行之中士聞道若存若亡下士聞道大笑之不笑不足以為道

故建言有之明道若昧進道若退夷道若纇上德若谷

大白若辱廣德若不足建德偷頁真若渝

大方無隅大器晚成大音希聲大象無形

道隱無名夫唯道善代貝且成

41

Difficulties

When a painter hears about the creative Tao,
she begins to put it in her landscapes.

When a singer hears of the creative Tao,
he sings it in his love songs.

When a poet hears of the creative Tao,
she rhymes her soul with it.

When a chef hears of the creative Tao,
he bakes it into his bread.

If it could not take infinite forms,
it would not be the creative Tao.
Difficulties find life in many forms.
The creative Tao gives life to all things.

Creativity 因

道生一生二二生三三生萬物萬物負陰而抱陽沖氣以為和

人之所惡唯孤寡不穀而王公以為稱故物或損之而益或益之而損

人之所教我亦教之強梁者不得其死吾將以為教父

共 Seclusion

42

Seclusion

One idea creates another. More ideas come from these.
Many things are possible.

All ideas combine the male and the female to create energy.
When energy is created, many things are possible.

Many people dislike seclusion.
The creative person can use it to form
connections with the universe.

When solitude is embraced, many things are possible.

Creativity 因

天下之至柔馳騁天下之至堅無有入無間

吾是以知無為之有益

不言之教無為之益天下希及之

柔 Without Words

86

43

Without Words

Empty space gives birth to forms.

Gentle creation is often overlooked.
When there are no words, silence can become deafening.

Creating without form; poetry without words.
The creative person lives her life.

Creativity 因

名與身孰親身與貨孰多得與亡孰病

是故甚愛必大費多藏必厚亡

知足不辱知止不殆可以長久

足 Rejection

Rejection

Shows and publications: are these important to you?
Profit or enjoyment: which matters the most?
Acceptance or rejection: how do you respond?

When you depend on others' praise,
you will always be empty.
If enjoyment depends only on profit,
you will often be disappointed.

When you are serene with your creative living and content
with the life you have, you realize that nothing is missing.

You know you belong to the universe.

大成若缺其用不弊大盈若沖其用不窮

大直若屈大巧若拙大辯若訥

躁勝寒靜勝熱清靜為天下正

45

Getting Out of the Way

Creating a life seems overwhelming.
Still, a life creates itself.

Filling up with living takes all of our time.
Innovation seems impossible.
Learning never ends.
A work of art is beyond us.

The creative person lets things happen.

When they happen, she folds them into her life.

Getting out of the way, she lives the creative Tao.

大下有道卻走馬以糞天下無道戎馬生於郊

禍莫大于可欲禍莫大于不知足咎莫大于欲得故至足之足常足矣

In Harmony with Your Times

46

In Harmony with Your Times

When you are in harmony with your times,
you see through the illusions.

Difficulties cause defensiveness and can create enemies.

When you can see through your fears,
you make your own safety.

Creativity 因

以是聖人不行而知不見而名不為而成

不出戶知天下不闚牖見天道其出彌遠其知彌少

 From the Inside Out

94

47

From the Inside Out

Within your circle, you are connected to the world.
By looking within, you can see the creative Tao.

When you seek to know more,
you find that you understand less.

The creative person understands this paradox.
He has visions with his eyes closed
and creates while doing nothing.

為學日益為道日損

損之又損以至於無為　無為而無不為

取天下常以無事及其有事不足以取天下

禮 Creating Less is Creating More

96

Creating Less is Creating More

When you seek knowledge, you add something everyday.
When you live the creative Tao, you drop something everyday.

Once you understand that you do not need to force things,
you see that less is more.

When you do nothing, you leave nothing undone.

A creative life unfolds when you
let things go their natural ways.
You cannot gain by creating more.

聖人無常心以百姓心為心善者吾善之

不善者吾亦善之德善

信者吾善信之不信者吾亦信之德信

聖人在天下歙歙為天下渾其心

百姓皆注其耳目聖人皆孩之

The Human Family

The creative person does not
impose her visions on other people.
Instead, she seeks to understand how others see.

She creates for people who are good,
and she also creates for those who are not.
This is how the creative person works.

She trusts that people will experience her work as they must,
in their own ways.
She imagines all people to be part of the human family.
In this way,
she shares her creativity and her connection with the universe.

夫何故以其無死地

兕無所投其角虎無所措其爪兵無所容其刃

蓋聞善攝生者陸行不遇兕虎入軍不被甲兵

夫何故以生生之厚

出生入死生之徒十有三死之徒十有三人之生動之死地亦十有三

Creating Toward Life

A creative person learns to be present to
whatever is presented in his life.

He understands that his life is temporary
and that eventually he will die.
Because he understands this,
he is able to create whatever he can,
using all that is available to him.

When his life is over,
he lets go and welcomes the next stage of his journey.

道生之德畜之物形之勢成之

是以万物莫不尊道而貴德

道之尊德之貴夫莫之命而常自然

故道生之德畜之長之育之亭之毒之養之覆之

生而不有為而不恃長而不宰是謂之德

母

The Tao and Creating

51

The Tao and Creating

The Tao creates all things in our world.
All forms are expressions of the Tao.

In the creative Tao,
there is support for continuing this expression.

There is space and silence and nurturing and comfort
through the necessary processes.

The Tao is not visible to the creative person,
but the creative person makes the Tao visible.

Creativity 因

天下有始以為天下母既知其母以知其子既知其子復守其母

没身不殆塞其兌開其門終身不勤開其兌濟其事終身不救

見小曰明守柔曰強用其光復歸其明無遺身殃是為習常

Telling the Story

Telling the Story

Each person has a story to tell.
When you know your own story,
you begin to understand your life.

If you refuse to know yourself,
you may limit your possibilities.
If you embrace your journey,
you may find peace in your heart.

Seeking the unknown helps to create mysteries.
Giving up the known may lead to enlightenment.
Telling the story is a creative person's quest.

使我介然有知行於大道唯施是畏

大道甚夷而民好徑

朝甚除田甚蕪倉甚虛服文綵帶利劍厭飲食

財貨有餘是謂盜夸非道也哉

53

Forms Are Powerful

Following the creative Tao is available to all,
yet many people avoid this possibility.

The creative way is elusive; remain in touch with your center.

Creativity is sometimes lost
when conformity and materialism are dominant.

To maintain the creative Tao, create forms that are unique;
these forms remind the others of their creative power.

One-of-a-kind forms touch our souls,
while manufactured products rob us of our dreams.

The original forms we create from imagination are our legacy.

善建者不拔善抱者不脱子孫以祭祀不輟

修之於身其德乃真修之於家其德乃餘

修之於鄉其德乃長修之於國其德乃豐

修之於天下其德乃普

故以身觀身以家觀家以鄉觀鄉以國觀國

以天下觀天下

吾何以知天下然哉以此

祖 Roots and Creating

Roots and Creating

Your roots provide the source for your creativity.
When you remember where you began,
you can continue to grow forward.

When the creative Tao is present in your living,
you create authenticity.

When it is part of your social support,
those around you will grow and prosper.
When it extends to your homeland and the universe,
growth and harmony are possible.

How can this be? Look at your roots
and imagine the growth of the tree.

含德之厚比於赤子蜂蠆虺蛇不螫猛獸不據攫鳥不搏

骨弱筋柔而握固未知牝牡之合而全作精之至也終日號而不嗄

和之至也知和曰常知常曰明

益生曰祥心使氣曰強物壯則老謂之不道不道早已

55

Beginnings

When you become aware of the creative Tao,
you create beginnings.

Like a new life, there is weakness, and there is also strength.
A seed when planted has no knowledge of
what it is to become.
Yet, it grows when nurtured and is transformed into something
that looks nothing like its beginnings.

The creative person is like a new beginning.
Without knowledge of the outcome, she begins her work.

Because the process matters most,
the outcomes never disappoint.

The creative person engages in beginnings
and is thus renewed.

知者不言言者不知塞其兑闭其门

挫其锐解其分和其光同其塵

是謂元同

故不可得而親不可得而疏不可得而利

不可得而害不可得而貴不可得而賤

故为天下贵

灵 Space Between the Forms

56

Space Between the Forms

Created forms speak for themselves.
Trying to explain them is not what they are.

Be patient and quiet, receptive and peaceful.

In stillness, receive the messages from the forms
and the spaces between the forms.

Be like the creative Tao. It is always there.
It cannot be captured or released, hurt or cared for,
rewarded or punished.

It endures because it lets go and is both space and form.

以正治國以奇用兵以無事取天下

吾何以知其然哉以此

天下多忌諱而民彌貧民多利器國家滋昏

人多伎巧奇物滋起法令滋彰盜賊多有

故聖人云我無為而民自化我好靜而民自正

我無事而民自富我無欲而民自樸

凡 Letting Go of Expectations

114

57

Letting Go of Expectations

When living the creative Tao, let go of your expectations.

Let your materials guide you in your work.

The more rules you make, the fewer will be your possibilities.
The more expectations you have,
the less freedom you will have.
The more you race with time, the less time you have.

The creative person lets go of expectations
and is surprised at the results.
She lets go of plans, and new works create themselves.
She lets go of her doubts and understands her process.

其政悶悶其民淳淳其政察察其民缺缺

禍兮福之所倚福兮禍之所伏孰知其極其無正

正復為奇善復為妖人之迷其日固久

是以聖人方而不割廉而不劌直而不肆光而不耀

Relaxed Attention

Relaxed Attention

The creative person cultivates a way of living
where he attends to the world in a relaxed way.

When opportunities for creativity present themselves,
he is ready.
When attention is forced, the results are contrived.
When you create in order to make others happy,
you risk your own happiness.

The creative person understands the importance of readiness.

He prepares his materials, integrates his mistakes,
and is ready for the unfolding opportunities.

治人事天莫若嗇夫唯嗇是謂早服早服謂之重積德

重積德則無不克無不克則莫知其極莫知其極可以有國

有國之母可以長久是謂根深柢固長生久視之道

59

Grist for the Mill

The creative person does not seek extremes.
She sees all of life as *grist for the mill.*

All things have possibility in living a creative life.

Staying free of patterns and routine,
she folds everything into her work.

Because there is no destination,
she welcomes all experiences along the way.
Because she lets go, she can receive all things.

Creativity 因

治大國若烹小鮮以道莅天下其鬼不神非其鬼不神

其神不傷人非其神不傷人聖人亦不傷人

夫兩不相傷故德交歸焉

 醸 Re-Creating

Re-Creating

The creative Tao does not require much work.
Too much attention changes the process
and may spoil the outcome.

The creative person who understands the Tao
will re-create her life and her work again and again.

By being in process, the creative person avoids the comments
of critics and dilutes the power of opponents.

大國者下流天下之交天下之牝

牝常以靜勝牡以靜為下

故大國以下小國則取小國小國以下大國則取大國故或下以取

或下而取大國不過欲並畜人小國不過欲入事人

夫兩者各得其所大者宜為下

A Work of Art

When someone creates a work of art, he may attract the
attention of others. Because of the attention,
the artist has a need for perspective.

By trusting the creative Tao,
the artist remains humble and respectful.

When perspective is lost,
the creative person realizes it and works to regain balance.

She admits her mistakes
and thanks those who inform her about them.
She knows that she can be her own worst enemy.

When a creative person follows the Tao,
she comes to understand that each of us is a work of art.

道者万物之奥善人之宝不善人之所保

美言可以市尊行可以加人人之不善何棄之有

故立天子置三公虽有拱璧以先駟馬不如坐進此道

古之所以貴此道者何不曰以求得有罪以免邪故为天下貴

听

In the Middle of the Tao

In the Middle of the Tao

The creative person stays centered in the Tao.
He knows this is available to all persons, good and bad.

Your creative works may be praised,
and people may purchase what you have created.

Being in the center of the Tao is beyond praise and purchase.

When students come to you to learn to be creative,
you cannot teach them what you know.

Instead, tell them about the creative Tao.
When they understand the Tao,
they will begin to create their own works.

In the middle of the Tao, all things are possible.

.

为无为事无事味无味大小多少报怨以德

图难于其易为大于其细天下难事必作于易

天下大事必作于细是以圣人终不为大故能成其大

夫轻诺必寡信多易必多难是以圣人犹难之

故终无难矣

淡 Writing without Words,
Painting without Brushes

63

Writing without Words, Painting without Brushes

Writing without words and painting without brushes.
How can this be so?

When the creative person is one with his work,
his work is accomplished with no effort.
Poems emerge as pictures, and pictures become poems.

Do not aspire to greatness, and greatness may come to you.

When an obstacle appears, stop and give yourself to it.

Do not worry about your comfort,
and you will become comfortable with your discomfort.

其安易持其未兆易谋其脆易泮其微易散为之于未有治之于未乱

合抱之木生于毫末九层之台起于累土千里之行始于足下

为者败之执者失之是以圣人无为故无败无执故无失

民之从事常于几成而败之慎终如始则无败事

是以圣人欲不欲不贵难得之货学不学复众人之所过

以辅万物之自然而不敢为

Avoiding Difficulties

When an idea is new, it is easy to nourish it.
When a song is beginning, it is easy to make changes.
Delicate works are easy to break. Small things scatter in the wind.

Prevent difficulties in your work before they begin.
Plan for the future before it arrives.

A symphony grows one note at a time.
Each dance begins with a single step.

Moving too soon, you stumble.
Holding the brush too tightly, you miss the point.
Working with deadlines, you may rush a project to completion.

The creative person
avoids difficulties by letting projects take their natural course.
She is as serene at the end as at the beginning.

Because she does not own her work,
she cannot have it stolen from her.
What she wants is to want nothing.

She has learned to unlearn.
She avoids difficulties by letting others be who they are.
She cares for the Tao and thus, for everything.

古之善為道者非以明民將以愚之民之難治以其智多

故以智治國國之賊不以智治國國之福

知此兩者亦稽式常知稽式是謂元德

元德深矣遠矣與物反矣然後乃至大順

Learning to Create

A creative person does not try to teach others to be creative.
Instead, she gently teaches them to know not.

When someone believes that they know how to be creative,
they are not available to create.

When someone knows that they know not,
they are following the creative Tao.

Learning to create does not come from being wealthy or wise.

Being clear and authentic, living a simple life,
the creative person may be an example to others
who will find their own paths to creation.

江海所以能为百谷王者以其善下之故能为百谷王

是以欲上民必以言下之欲先民必以身後之

是以聖人处上而民不重处前而民不害

是以天下乐推而不厭以其不争故天下莫能与之争

Being Humble

Everything returns to the earth,
because it is the mother of everything.
The earth is humble and powerful in its receptivity.

To be a creative leader,
you must practice humbleness and support others in the
ways that the earth supports all things.

Following is a powerful way to lead.

The creative person does not take advantage of others
or oppress them in their learning.

Because he does not compete in his creativity,
there is no way to compete with him.

天下皆謂我道大似不肖夫唯大故似不肖若肖久矣其細也夫

我有三寶持而保之一曰慈二曰儉三曰不敢為天下先

慈故能勇儉故能廣不敢為天下先故能成器長

今舍慈且勇舍儉且廣舍後且先死矣

夫慈以戰則勝以守則固天將救之以慈衛之

Three Guideposts for Creativity

Three Guideposts for Creativity

You may think that the creative Tao is naive or without merit.

If you have considered how you live a creative life,
you may find succor in it.
If you are able to live a creative life,
you will find the source of this way.

There are three guideposts to consider for creativity:
openness, not judging, playfulness.

When you are open to your experiences,
you reach for the source of your creativity.

When you do not judge your work,
you allow your creativity to unfold from its center.

In playfulness, you are able to make your work
an experience of play and pleasure.

善为士者不武善戰者不怒善勝敵者不與

善用人者为之下是謂不爭之德

是謂用人之力是謂配天古之極

Playful Ink

The dancer moves in harmony with others.
The musician brings her music to an audience
while pleasing herself.
The playwright and actors
capture the essence of daily drama.
The poet draws words with playful ink.

Creative people embody the many possibilities of human expression.

Without competition,
they create in the spirit of play and celebration.
Like children, they are within the creative Tao.

用兵有言吾不敢為主而為客不敢進寸而退尺

是謂行無行攘無臂扔無敵執無兵

禍莫大于輕敵輕敵幾喪吾寶故抗兵相加哀者勝矣

耐 Honoring Others

Honoring Others

When looking at the creative works of others,
be open and experience what is given to you.
It is not necessary to compare your work with theirs.

By honoring others,
you have the opportunity to step back from your work.

When the creative person makes room to learn from the
work of others, he does not need to battle with himself.

By yielding, he understands victory.

吾言甚易知甚易行天下莫能知莫能行
言有宗事有君夫唯無知是以不我知
知我者希則我者貴是以聖人被褐懷玉

70

Finding Your Way

If you want to understand the creative Tao,
relax and let go of trying.

This wisdom has always been with us,
yet we often fail to understand it.

The way to finding your way is to follow your heart.

知不知上不知不知病夫唯病病是以不病聖人不病以其病病

是以不病

 Shifting Shapes

71

Shifting Shapes

Nothing stays the same. Shifting shapes remind us of this.

When this fluidity contains life, then life becomes whole.

The creative person becomes whole by following the changes and welcoming them into her life.

民不畏威則大威至

無狎其所居無厭其所生夫唯不厭是以不厭

是以聖人自知不自見自愛不自貴故去彼取此

模 Awe-Full Creating

144

72

Awe-Full Creating

The creative person embraces the awe-full
and gives form to the formless.

If this cannot be done,
then those in authority become powerful.

When a creative person understands this, she creates distance
from authority. In this way, she helps others see the difference,
and they begin to understand.

勇於敢則殺勇於不敢則活此兩者或利或害

天之所惡孰知其故是以聖人猶難之

天之道不爭而善勝不言而善應不召而自來

繟然而善謀天網恢恢疏而不失

Universal Themes

The creative Tao is comfortable.
It survives without dominance;
expresses without sound;
presents without invitation;
and creates without effort.

Its themes are universal,
and the Tao holds everything safe in its circle.

民不畏死奈何以死懼之

若使民常畏死而為奇者吾得執而殺之孰敢

常有司殺者殺夫代司殺者殺是謂代大匠斲

夫代大匠斲者希有不傷其手矣

換 The Changing Universe

The Changing Universe

Change is ever-present. Nothing lasts.
The creative person recognizes this
and does not try to interfere.

Because he does not struggle to control these changes,
he does not damage the work he does.

Instead, he transforms the inevitable
and makes himself a part of the changing universe.

民之饑以其上食稅之多是以饑民之難治以其上之有為是以難治

民之輕死以其上求生之厚是以輕死夫唯無以生為者是賢於貴生

Accessible Creativity

When the world is out of balance, people are restless.
When pushed too hard,
people become hostile and depressed.

Access your creativity
and encourage others to access theirs as well.

When you trust others, they begin to trust themselves.

人之生也柔弱其死也堅強萬物草木之生也柔脆

其死也枯槁故堅強者死之徒柔弱者生之徒

是以兵強則不勝木強則兵強大處下柔弱處上

敏 Always Another Opportunity

76

Always Another Opportunity

A creative life has many ups and downs.
There is always another opportunity to choose.

By being flexible and receptive,
the creative person learns to yield
to the ebb and flow of the universe.

By resisting this energy, a life becomes stagnant.

By embracing it, there is always another opportunity.

Creativity 因

天之道其猶張弓與高者抑之下者舉之

有餘者損之不足者補之

天之道損有餘而補不足人之道則不然損不足以奉有餘

孰能有餘以奉天下唯有道者

是以聖人為而不恃功成而不處其不欲見賢

稳

Doing Your Part

154

Doing Your Part

To bring balance to your life, take time to do your part.

The creative person adjusts her work
so she gives and receives in the process of creation.

Those who take it all,
who are hungry for power, do not know the Tao.
They keep the world out of balance.

The creative person
can continue her work because her resources are renewable.

She takes herself lightly and does not hold herself above others.

天下莫柔弱於水而攻堅弱者莫之能勝以其無以易之

弱之勝強柔之勝剛天下莫不知莫能行

是以聖人云受國之垢是謂社稷主受國不祥

是為天下王正言若反

女 Innocent Creating

78

Innocent Creating

To live a creative life is to be as pliable and fluid as water.
Over time, a creative life wears down rocks
and other objects in its path.

By creating innocently, the unknown becomes the known.
Images emerge from unexpected sources.

The creative person stays centered in his life
and remains innocent in his work.

Because he does not try to impress others,
others are impressed with his creations.

There is truth in innocence.

和大怨必有餘怨安可以為善是以聖人執左契

而不責於人有德司契無德司徹

天道無親常與善人

責 Correcting Mistakes

158

79

Correcting Mistakes

Whenever mistakes are made,
there is the possibility of learning something new.

If others are blamed, the mistakes continue.

To live a creative life,
take the opportunities presented by your mistakes.

In this way, you will learn what is necessary,
and others are free to do this also.

小國寡民使有什伯之器而不用
使民重死而不遠徙雖有舟輿無所乘之
雖有甲兵無所陳之使人復結繩而用之
甘其食美其服安其居乐其俗
鄰國相望鷄犬之声相聞
民至老死不相往来

不

The Grass is Not Greener

80

The Grass is Not Greener

If you enjoy your life and your work, you will be content.

Creating a life does not require diversions.

You may leave home to see other places or to visit friends.
You may know of far away places and exotic ways of living.

When you know that the grass is not greener elsewhere,
you can live and die in your own place
and know that you have led a full life.

信言不美美言不信善者不辯辯者不善知者不博博者不知

聖人不積既以為人己愈有既以與人己愈多

天之道利而不害聖人之道為而不爭

81

Creating and the Tao

Creative works seem simple,
but simplicity is not always creative.

The creative person does not need to draw attention.
Works that draw attention are not always creative.

The creative person has no need to possess.
By giving away what she has, she has more than enough.

The Tao creates by nurturing.

By not conforming,
the creative person creates her life and makes it her own.

Bibliography

Bedford, Mitchell. *Existentialism and Creativity*. New York: Philosophical Library, Inc., 1972.

Belenky, Mary, et al. *Women's Ways of Knowing: The Development of Self, Voice and Mind*. New York: Basic Books, Harper Collins, 1986.

Bolen, Jean Shinoda. *The Tao of Psychology*. New York: Harper and Row, Publishers, Inc., 1979.

Breathnach, Sarah. *Simple Abundance*. New York: Warner Books, Inc., 1995.

Brown, Rita Mae. *Starting From Scratch*. New York: Bantam Books, 1988.

Cameron, Julia. *The Artist's Way*. New York: Jeremy P. Tarcher/Perigee Books, 1992.

Campbell, Joseph. *The Hero With a Thousand Faces*. Princeton: Princeton University Press, 1949.

Capra, Fritjof. *The Tao of Physics*. New York: Bantam Books, 1975.

Capra, Fritjof. *Uncommon Wisdom*. New York: Simon and Schuster, 1988.

Dalton, Jerry. *The Tao Te Ching: Backwards Down the Path*. Atlanta, Georgia: Humanics New Age, 1994.

Dillard, Annie. *The Writing Life*. New York: Harper and Row Publishers, 1989.

Edwards, Betty. *Drawing on the Right Side of the Brain*. Los Angeles: J. P. Tarcher, Inc., 1979.

Epel, Naomi. *Writers Dreaming*. New York: Vintage Books, 1993.

Feng, Gia-Fu and Jane English. *Lao Tsu: Tao Te Ching*. New York: Vintage Books, 1972.

Fields, Rick et al. *Chop Wood Carry Water*. Los Angeles: Jeremy P. Tarcher, 1984.

Fulghum, Robert. *All I Really Need to Know I Learned in Kindergarten*. New York: Villard Books, 1988.

Gardner, Howard. *Creating Minds*. New York: Basic Books, 1993.

Gardner, Howard. *Frames of Mind*. New York: Basic Books, 1983.

Gawain, Shakti. *Creative Visualization*. Mill Valley, California: Whatever Publishing, 1986.

Ghiselin, Brewster, ed. *The Creative Process*. California: University of California Press, 1952.

Goldberg, Natalie. *Long Quiet Highway*. New York: Bantam Books, 1993.

Goldberg, Natalie. *Wild Mind*. New York: Bantam Books, 1990.

Goldberg, Natalie. *Writing Down the Bones*. Boston: Shambhala, 1986.

Grigg, Ray. *The Tao of Being: A Think and Do Workbook*. Atlanta, Georgia: Humanics New Age, 1994.

Heider, John. *The Tao of Leadership*. Atlanta, Georgia: Humanics New Age, 1986.

Heilbrun, Carolyn. *Writing a Woman's Life*. New York: Ballantine Books, 1990.

Heus, Michael and Allen Pincus. *The Creative Generalist*. Barneveld, Wisconsin: Micamar Publishing, 1986.

Hoff, Benjamin. *The Tao of Pooh*. New York: Penguin Books, 1982.

Hoff, Benjamin. *The Te of Piglet*. New York: Dutton, 1992.

Kawasaki, Guy. *Hindsights*. New York: Warner Books, Inc., 1993.

Lamott, Anne. *Bird By Bird*. New York: Pantheon Books, 1994.

Laing, R. D. Knots. New York: Vintage Books, 1970.

Maslow , Abraham. *The Farther Reaches of Human Behavior*. New York: The Viking Press, 1971.

May, Rollo. *The Courage to Create*. New York: Bantam Books, 1975.

Metz, Pamela. *The Tao of Learning*. Atlanta, Georgia: Humanics New Age, 1994.

Metz, Pamela and Jacqueline Tobin. *The Tao of Women*. Atlanta Georgia: Humanics Limited, 1995.

Mitchell, Stephen. *Tao te Ching*. New York: Harper and Row Publishers, Inc., 1988.

Nachmanovitch, Stephen. *Free Play*. Los Angeles: Jeremy P. Tarcher, 1991.

Quinn, Daniel. *Ishmael*. New York: Bantam Books, 1992.

Rilke, Rainer Maria. *Letters to a Young Poet*. New York: Vintage Books, 1984.

Shank, Roger. *The Creative Attitude*. New York: Macmillan Publishing Company, 1988.

Shekerjian, Denise. *Uncommon Genius*. New York: Penguin Books, 1990.

Shuman, Sandra. *Source Imagery*. New York: Doubleday, 1989.

Signell, Karen. *Wisdom of the Heart*. New York: Bantam Books, 1990.

Sinetar, Marsha. *Ordinary People as Monks and Mystics*. New York: Paulist Press, 1986.

Smith, D. Howard. *The Wisdom of the Taoists*. New York: New Directions Books, 1980.

St. James, Elaine. *Inner Simplicity*. New York: Hyperion, 1995.

St. James, Elaine. *Simplify Your Life*. New York: Hyperion, 1994.

Starhawk. *The Spiral Dance*. New York: Harper and Row, 1979.

Stevens, Edward. *Spiritual Technologies*. New York: Paulist Press, 1990.

Stevens, John. *Awareness: exploring, experimenting, experiencing*. Lafayette, California: Real People Press, 1971.

Suzuki, Shunryu. *Zen Mind, Beginner's Mind*. New York: Weatherhill, 1970.

Sweet, Robert. *Writing Towards Wisdom*. California: Helios House, 1990.

Vaughan, Frances. *Awakening Intuition*. New York: Anchor Books, 1979.

Watts, Alan. *Tao: The Watercourse Way*. New York: Pantheon Books, 1975.

Whyte, David. *The Heart Aroused*. New York: Doubleday, 1994.

Wing, R. L. *The Illustrated I Ching*. New York: Doubleday and Company, Inc., 1982.

Wing, R. L. *The Tao of Power*. New York: Doubleday and Company, Inc., 1986.

Wonder, Jacquelyn and Priscilla Dovovan. *Whole Brain Thinking*. New York: Ballantine Books, 1984.

About the Author

Pamela Metz lives in Denver, Colorado where she is the associate dean of academic and student affairs at the University of Denver Graduate School of Social Work. She holds degrees in education and social work from Illinois State University, the University of Denver and the University of Colorado. Dr. Metz has taught in university settings, public and private schools, and the innovative University Without Walls. She has worked as an elementary teacher, hospice social worker and educational administrator. Living a creative and creating life through the wisdom of the Tao is part of her unfolding path.

40017563R00102

Made in the USA
Middletown, DE
31 January 2017